Essay: Computer Viruses

Sirinya Pakditawan

GRIN

Bibliographic information published by the German National Library:

The German National Library lists this publication in the National Bibliography; detailed bibliographic data are available on the Internet at http://dnb.dnb.de.

ISBN: 9783656983897
This book is also available as an ebook.

Nymphenburger Straße 86
80636 München

Print and binding: Books on Demand GmbH, Norderstedt, Germany
Printed on acid-free paper from responsible sources.

GRIN web shop: https://www.grin.com/document/186203

Advanced Integrated Skills

WS 2001/2002

Sirinya Pakditawan

Computer Viruses: History, Reasons and Effects on Society

Content

1. Abstracts

Since the beginning of the internet age in the early 1980s, people have not merely been concerned with keeping the internet free from viruses. In point of fact, some people wreak havoc on the internet by creating and spreading nasty and disastrous computer viruses. Hence, the so-called hackers[1] cause mayhem and destruction in the net. It is a fact that computer viruses cause great damage because they can pass from one computer to another like a biological virus, thus infecting the system.

Hence, a computer virus can be regarded as the undesirable embodiment of human intelligence to interrupt and to create a vacuum in the constant flow of internet information. What is more, the history of the computer virus is laced with the human need to be recognized. Thus, many research projects show that the majority of virus creators crave public acknowledgement. However, there are many other reasons why people try to spread computer viruses. Nonetheless, all hackers can be seen as dangerous and harmful, being indifferent to the consequences of spreading viruses to themselves and to others.

In the following, I will concentrate on the phenomenon of computer viruses. Therefore, I will focus on the reasons why computer viruses were brought to life, discussing the history of the computer virus and the effects it has taken on our society. It is a fact that hackers not only use viruses, worms[2] and Trojan horses[3] to cause a loss of information but also to gain control over remote systems and the information stored on these systems. For this reason, I will not only concentrate on the way the virus affects our everyday life but also on the effects it has in the business sector.

---

[1] "Hacker" is the informal expression for a person who tries to gain access to the contents of a computer's memory without permission.

[2] A worm is a piece of software that makes copies of itself by using computer networks and security flaws. In other words, a worm replicates itself to a computer using the security flaw and then begins replicating. Cf. Computer virus. http://en.wikipedia.org/wiki/Computer_virus.

[3] A Trojan horse is simply a computer program that pretends to do one thing but actually causes damage to the computer when it is started. In contrast to a worm, a Trojan horse cannot replicate automatically. Cf. ibid.

2. Computer Viruses: History, Reasons and Effects on Society

In the late 1980s, with the beginning of the internet age, traditional computer viruses were mostly first seen. There are some reasons why they came about at that time. The first and the most important reason was the spread of personal computers. In fact, PCs became very popular in the 1980s and thus became very common in homes, businesses and college campuses.[4] Hence, the personal computer has nearly become omnipotent.

Another reason that led to the evolution of computer viruses in the late 1980s was the use of bulletin boards on the computer.[5] As bulletin board systems became quite popular in the late 1980s and early 1990s, more viruses were created to infect popularly traded software. Thus, bulletin boards primarily led to what is today known as the so-called Trojan horse.[6] The third reason why computer viruses came about at that time was most definitely the use of the floppy disk. As programs were still very small at the end of the 1980s, all kind of data could be fit on a single floppy disk and transferred to other computers. Hence, viruses could also be transmitted from one PC to another via floppy disk.

Thus, in 1986 one of the first computer viruses ever written, "The Brain", was released by the brothers Basit and Amjad Farooq Alvi in Lahore, Pakistan.[7] What is more, since Robert Morris unleashed a worm that invaded ARPANET computers, experts have tried to make economic as well as ethical and moral sense of the event. The small program that Morris created disabled about 6,000 computers on the network by flooding their memory banks with copies of itself. According to A. Ross this virus and other similar attacks on the internet

---

[4] It is a fact that prior to the 1980s PCs were very rare and thus nearly non-existent. The computers that some people did have at home were mostly toys. Cf. Computer viruses, p. 2.

[5] People could easily download all sorts of different programs from a bulletin board. Most popular were games. Cf. ibid.

[6] Cf. note 3.

[7] Cf. Computer viruses, p. 2 and Brian Krebs. A Short History of Computer Viruses and Attacks. http://www.washingtonpost.com/ac2/wp-dyn/A50635-2002Jun26?start=15&per=18.

has helped "to generate a moral panic that has all but transformed everyday "computer culture"".[8]

As a response to the internet virus spread by Morris, anti-virus centers were founded, for instance, by government and defence agencies such as the National Science Foundation, the NASA and the Energy Department.[9] In addition, plans were made to replace the 1986 Computer Fraud and Abuse Act[10] by the more severe Computer Virus Eradication Act which would sentence hackers up to ten years of prison.[11] What is more, people also called for the creation of a Center for Virus Control similar to the Atlanta's Centers for Disease Control.[12]

In the media, the computer virus has often been compared to sexually transmitted diseases such as the Aids virus, but also to a cholera epidemic. Hence, the media urged people's attention to "personal systems hygiene".[13] In point of fact, there are many similarities between the Aids and the internet virus for both take over the host cell and the program respectively and replicate the viruses. Thus, the biological and the electronic virus spread by inserting itself into living cells.[14] Hence, one can say that both kinds of viruses need host cells.

However, there is also a fundamental difference between the biological and the electronic virus. As A. Ross notes "[i]n contrast to HIV's lack of meaning or intentionality, the meaning of cybernetic viruses is always already replete with social significance".[15] In fact, computer viruses do carry meaning because people have various reasons for creating them. What is more, computer viruses are mostly *deliberately* created by programmers. Hence, unlike

---

[8] Andrew Ross. Hacking away at the Counterculture. http://www.3.iath.virginia.edu/pme/text-only/issue.990/ross-1.990.
[9] Cf. ibid.
[10] This act was only relevant to government information. Cf. ibid, p. 2.
[11] In fact, people have called for a new criminal legislation which will define crimes with computers as a special category of crime. Thus, people claimed that such crimes deserve extraordinary punitive measures.
[12] Cf. ibid, p. 1.
[13] Cf. ibid, pp. 2-3.
[14] Cf. ibid, p. 3 and Computer virus, p. 1.
[15] A. Ross, pp. 5-6.

biological viruses, internet viruses do not develop gradually and naturally by themselves.

Even today the image of the virus creator is still that of a young student who has the means to do it and something to prove himself and his peer group. In point of fact, virus writers are not a homogenous group of individuals. As J. Twist emphasizes by referring to S. Gordon, a renowned expert in security technology, "[t]he kind of person who creates such disruption differs in age, income, location, social/peer interaction, educational level, likes, dislikes and communication style (...)".[16] Hence, there are various reasons for spreading malicious software: viruses have been written as research projects, "jokes" and vandalism. Some virus writers also regard virus writing as a creative hobby, calling their creations works of art.

Thus, not all computer viruses are actually harmful. There are, in fact, some "good viruses" that are either intended to spread improvements to the programs they infect or to delete other viruses. Nonetheless, "good viruses" are quite rare and also habor danger in themselves, for if a "good virus" is poorly written it might misidentify its target file, thus removing a system file accidentally. Furthermore, releasing "good viruses" is nevertheless also a crime[17] because their creators usually operate without asking for permission of the computer owner, thus violating his private sphere.[18]

Nonetheless, there is an increasingly sinister side to those who wreak havoc on the internet. In fact, the organised crime element grows as virus writers are increasingly interested in hacking into computers in order to steal confidential information for profit.[19] It is a fact that spammers employ the best virus writers to help them. For this reason, a programmer might profit from whoever is using his Trojans as a source for spamming. Hence, Paul Wood, the chief security analyst at MessageLabs also told the BBC News Online that "they [virus

[16] Jo Twist. Why people write computer viruses. http://news.bbc.co.uk/go/pr/fr/-/1/hi/technology//3172967.stm.

[17] The subject of computer viruses as crimes is extendedly treated by Kerstin Mühle. *Hacker und Computer-Viren im Internet – eine strafrechtliche Beurteilung.* Dissertation, Passau 1998.

[18] Cf. Computer viruses, p. 3.

[19] Cf. J. Twist, p. 1.

writers] are becoming very advanced now in organised hi-tech criminal activity".[20]

As a matter of fact, some virus creators are indeed hi-tech criminals because they sell people the virus as a one-time only immunization shot along with its antidote.[21] These "virus vendors" are primarily motivated by financial gain. By selling viruses along with not very reliable antidotes, they take advantage of the already fast-growing sectors of the security system industry. Hence, hacking as such has also got a growing criminal connotation. As a consequence this has also "displaced the more innocuous, amateur mischief-maker-cum-media-star role reserved for hackers until a few years ago",[22] says A. Ross.

Even though the virus crisis led to a paranoid climate of privatization, hacking has had also a beneficial influence on information technology and society in general. In fact, hacking has been responsible for some of the most progressive developments in the innovation of software. Hence, hacking also contributed to uncovering security deficiencies as well as design flaws. And last but not least, speaking with A. Ross, the creation of computer viruses "is essential to the task of maintaining fronts of cultural resistance and stocks of oppositional knowledge as a hedge against a technofascist future".[23]

In conclusion, one might say that although there are some similarities between a biological and an electronic virus, computer viruses cannot come into existence spontaneously. They need to be deliberately created by programmers or by people who use virus creation software. Thus, a computer virus nearly always carries meaning because usually people do not spread viruses for fun or out of boredom.[24] Mostly they have some financial interests and try to take advantage of the "viral hysteria". Nevertheless, virus creators

---

[20] Cf. ibid.
[21] Cf. A. Ross, p. 8.
[22] Ibid, p. 10.
[23] Ibid.
[24] However, some virus creators do not seem to have "good" reasons for spreading viruses. Thus, one might say that they have similar motives to vandals who deliberately destroy or damage works of art, public or private property for no good reason. Cf. J. Twist, p. 2.

generally have in common that they long for public acknowledgement thus raising their self-esteem.

3. Bibliography

Computer virus. http://en.wikipedia.org/wiki/Computer_virus.

Krebs, Brian. *A Short History of Computer Viruses and Attacks.* http://www.washingtonpost.com/ac2/wp-dyn/A50635-2002Jun26?start=15&per=18.

Mühle, Kerstin. *Hacker und Computer-Viren im Internet – eine strafrechtliche Beurteilung.* Dissertation, Passau 1998.

Ross, Andrew. *Hacking away at the Counterculture.* http://www.3.iath.virginia.edu/pme/text-only/issue.990/ross-1.990.

Twist, Jo. *Why people write computer viruses.* http://news.bbc.co.uk/go/pr/fr/-/1/hi/technology//3172967.stm.